It's Time to Learn About Diabetes

A Workbook on Diabetes
for Children

Jean Betschart, MN, RN, CDE

It's Time to Learn About Diabetes

A Workbook on Diabetes for Children

by Jean Betschart, MN, RN, CDE

Illustrations by Nancy Songer, RN, MSN, CPNP

The development of this work was wholly supported by a grant from the Diabetes Research and Education Foundation, Bridgewater, New Jersey.

Provided to you as an Educational Service of
Boehringer Mannheim Corporation and Eli Lilly and Company

Opinions expressed in this book are those of the author, who firmly believes diabetes management should be individualized. This workbook should be used in conjunction with the advice of the child's doctor and other health professionals. Guidelines provided for target blood sugar levels and other topics should be discussed with the child's health professional team before incorporation into a daily management plan. Recommendations based on individual needs may be different from those stated here.

Acknowledgments

I greatly appreciate the support and encouragement of my colleagues in the Department of Endocrinology of Children's Hospital of Pittsburgh. I extend a special note of gratitude to Linda Siminerio, RN, MS, CDE, and Terri Yeager, RN, MSN, CRNP, CDE, for their interest in this project and especially to Nancy Songer, RN, MSN, CPNP, for her creative ideas and wonderful illustrations.

In addition, I want to thank the children who piloted the workbook and their families. They gave me "real" information on what a workbook should include!

I also am totally grateful for the loving support of my husband and family. Their tolerance of my endeavors has made it possible for me to find the time to complete the work.

Reviewers:

Dorothy Becker, MBBCH, FCD
Diane Betschart, teacher
James Betschart, DMD, MS, PhD
Barbara Bodnar, RN, BSN, CDE
Theresa Byrd, RN, CDE
Pat Carroll, MD
CHP Patient-Parent Education Committee
Louisa Cohen, teacher
Patricia Cooper, teacher and parent
Lynn Crowe
Emma D'Antonio, RN, PhD
Kathleen Dwyer, RD, PhD
Nancy Johncola, RN, CDE
Tom Lantz, teacher and parent
Margretta Lockard, teacher
Melinda Maryniuk, RD, CDE
JoAnne Moore, RN, BSN, CDE
Anita Nucci, RD
Noreen Papathoradeau, MSW
Sandra Puczynski, RN, MS, CDE
Max Salas, MD
Linda Siminerio, RN, MS, CDE
Linda Steranchak, CDE
Terri Yeager, RN, MSN, CRNP, CDE

Table of Contents

Unit V: During Special Times

Unit VI: On My Own

To the Teacher ...

As an educator, nurse, dietitian or related professional, you have an instrumental role in shaping the lives of children with diabetes. This workbook is intended to enhance your role by serving to supplement classroom learning.

This is a level I book, intended for use by the newly diagnosed child with insulin dependent diabetes mellitus. It is targeted for children ages 8 to 10 years, or second through fourth grade who are performing at grade level without learning disabilities or developmental delay. The content will serve to reinforce classroom learning and is not intended to replace classroom experiences.

Each chapter builds on previous knowledge. Optimal learning will take place if the chapters are completed consecutively.

You, as an educator, should use discretion regarding the use of this workbook in terms of the length and intensity of assignments. Units or chapters might be assigned as homework between education sessions. It is unlikely that most children would be able to complete the workbook during the initial hospitalization.

Your student will most likely learn best if you take time to either work through the exercises or review them with the child. As teachers, we never fail to learn from our students' responses.

To the Parent . . .

Your task is a difficult one when it comes to creating a physically, mentally and emotionally healthy environment for your child. Sometimes compromises must be made with a sacrifice in one area to compliment a need in another.

This workbook is intended to help to promote independence in your child. Knowledge of diabetes management is the first step in achieving independence. However, it is most important to keep in mind that children develop at very different rates. Therefore, what one child is able to accomplish at a given age, another child quite appropriately will not be able to do.

Encouraging your child to participate in his own self-care should not affect diabetes control. Supervision, involvement, continued interest and encouragement are still important at all ages. Your child should not be expected to independently take care of his diabetes. Parental involvement has been shown to positively affect diabetes control.

If you are able to help your child work through this workbook or discuss chapters after your child does them, his or her learning and awareness of your interest will be that much greater.

Important Phone Numbers

Doctor _____

Diabetes Educator _____

Dietitian _____

Pharmacy _____

Emergency _____

Child's Insulin Brand and Type _____

Size of Syringes _____

Meter _____

Strips _____

To the Student . . .

My name is Cindy and this is my friend Mike. We have diabetes. We're going to be your helpers as you do this workbook. We like knowing about diabetes so we can take care of ourselves and feel good! We know you're going to learn a lot. We sure did!

Your friends,

Cindy Mike

Cindy and Mike

Name _____   Date _____

Chapter 1.

Diabetes: How Did I Get It?

Your body is made up of many parts. Each part works with the others to keep you healthy. Sometimes one part of your body may not work as well as it should. When this happens, you might not feel well.

See if you know what your body parts do. I didn't!

One part of your body, called your pancreas, has many jobs. One job the pancreas does is to make insulin.

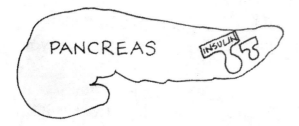

You will learn a lot about insulin in this workbook!

Look at the picture of some of the body parts inside you

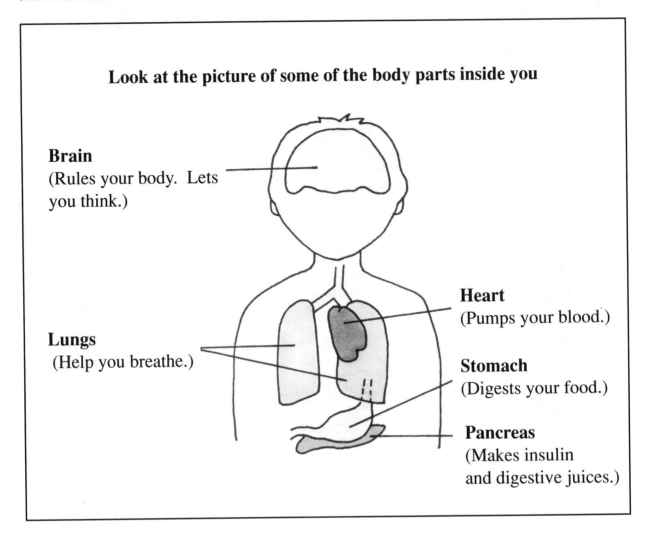

Brain
(Rules your body. Lets
you think.)

Lungs
(Help you breathe.)

Heart
(Pumps your blood.)

Stomach
(Digests your food.)

Pancreas
(Makes insulin
and digestive juices.)

Answer these questions:

1. What body part lets you think?_____

2. What body part digests your food? _____

3. What body part makes insulin and digestive juices?_____

4. What body part helps you breathe? _____

5. What body part pumps your blood? _____

**Draw the heart, lungs, stomach, brain, and pancreas
in the body outline below.
Write the names of each part and draw a line to it.**

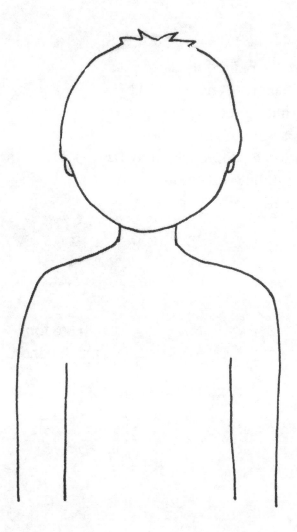

When your pancreas stops making insulin, <u>you have diabetes.</u>

What is the name of the illness that happens when your
pancreas stops making insulin? _____

You didn't do anything to cause your
diabetes. Diabetes is not caused by
eating or drinking too much sugar.
Sometimes a cold or flu can bring on
diabetes in some people who may be
going to get it, but you couldn't have
stopped diabetes from happening.

WRONG!

I could
have stopped it.

I ate too
much candy.

I was bad so I
got diabetes.

Circle the correct answer.

1. When you get diabetes, which body part has stopped making insulin?

       Lung   Heart   Pancreas   Stomach

2. Could you have kept yourself from getting diabetes?

       Yes   No

3. What can sometimes bring on diabetes in people who may be going to get it?

       Eating sugar   Drinking sugar   A cold or flu

Let's stay healthy.

Name _____ Date _____

Diabetes: What does it mean?

Even when you have diabetes, most of your pancreas is working just fine. Only one small part of your pancreas stops making insulin.

Insulin helps your body use food to give you energy. You need energy to do all the things you do every day, like go to school and play.

People who have diabetes must do special things to take good care of themselves so they will stay healthy.

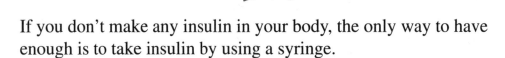

If you don't make any insulin in your body, the only way to have enough is to take insulin by using a syringe.

Taking insulin really is OK! Sometimes you might not feel a thing when you take your insulin, but other times you might feel a little pinch.

You will need to try to eat your meals and snacks on time. It is also important to eat well-balanced meals and snacks. Most foods that don't have too much sugar or too much fat are OK to eat.

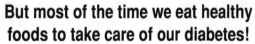

People with diabetes need to check their blood for sugar
and their urine (pee) for ketones. We'll tell you more
about ketones a little later.

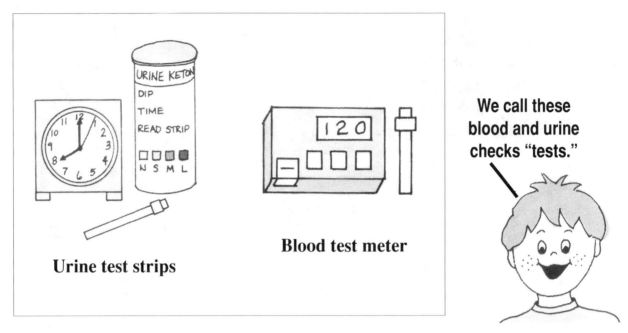

Urine test strips   **Blood test meter**

We call these
blood and urine
checks "tests."

It is important for you to learn how to do the test
exactly right and to write down the numbers you get.

Don't forget
to write them down!

When children with diabetes take care of themselves, they feel healthy and grow just fine.

If you have diabetes, you can play in all sports and activities! In fact, they are good for you!

Circle 5 things that children with diabetes should do to take good care of themselves.

Skip meals   Take insulin

Test blood   Eat on time

Eat fatty foods   Test urine

Write down your blood and urine sugar numbers

In this puzzle, find these words:

INSULIN   PANCREAS   SUGAR   DIABETES
URINE   TEST   SYRINGE   HEALTHY
NEEDLE   BODY   FAT   SNACKS
STOMACH

```
U  D  T  W  N  V  X  S  O  Q  P  T  E  S  T
S  I  C  N  P  F  Q  L  S  A  P  E  E  W  Y
T  A  O  P  A  Z  X  C  N  B  G  M  K  H  G
O  B  Y  S  U  G  A  R  G  N  Q  S  P  O  I
M  E  O  N  B  G  F  T  I  A  S  D  A  S  C
A  T  N  D  Z  A  P  R  O  W  I  E  N  N  T
C  E  L  J  Y  M  Y  C  X  Z  A  S  C  E  G
H  S  K  L  P  S  O  E  S  S  V  Q  R  E  I
Q  U  I  H  G  I  N  S  U  L  I  N  E  D  H
A  S  R  I  D  C  X  V  B  N  M  N  A  L  Z
M  N  O  I  V  C  S  N  A  C  K  S  S  E  W
L  K  F  H  N  S  O  O  I  E  R  T  W  E  F
D  M  A  Y  X  E  J  I  K  P  L  T  Q  R  E
S  Y  T  H  E  A  L  T  H  Y  B  N  G  H  M
K  L  O  Z  Q  S  D  S  F  G  H  I  W  X  A
```

Name _____ Date _____

Chapter 2.

What Happens When You Get Diabetes?

This is a picture of a pancreas. One job of the pancreas is to make insulin.

Did you know that your whole body is made up of cells?

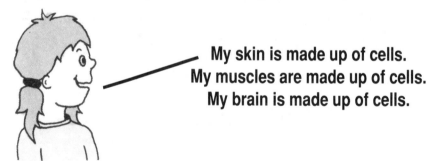

My skin is made up of cells.
My muscles are made up of cells.
My brain is made up of cells.

Cells are so small we can't see them with our eyes. Cells might look like this when you look through a microscope.

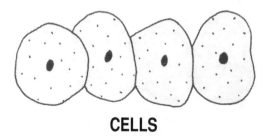

CELLS

Cells are alive because our bodies are alive! But they need to have sugar in order to live. Cells don't eat pizza, apples, or cheese. They eat the sugar made from all the food you eat! Insulin lets the sugar get inside the cells of your body. This is what gives you energy to run, play, think, and do everything you do!

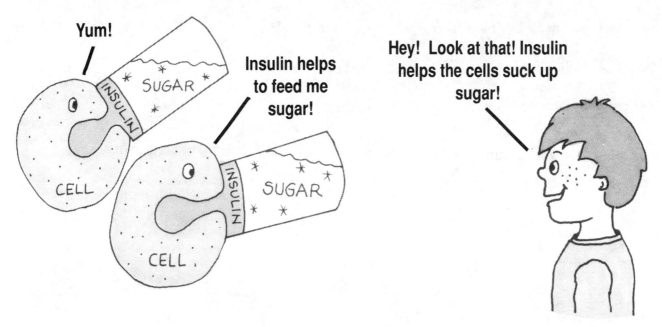

Each cell can eat when insulin helps sugar from the food you eat get inside. When cells are able to eat, they are happy.

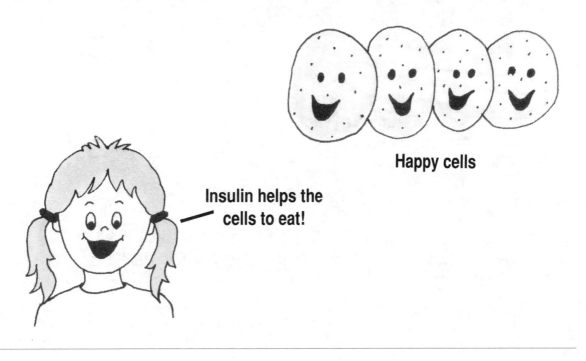

Fill in the missing letters for these words.

1. This body part makes insulin.   __ __ N __ R __ A __

2. Your body is made up of these.   __ __ L L __

3. Not made by your pancreas when you have diabetes. __ __ S U __ I __

4. Cells need to eat __ U G __ __ to live.

We're hungry!

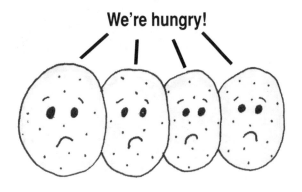

When you get diabetes, your pancreas stops making insulin. When your body cells can't eat, they are unhappy.

Cells are starving. Eat more food!

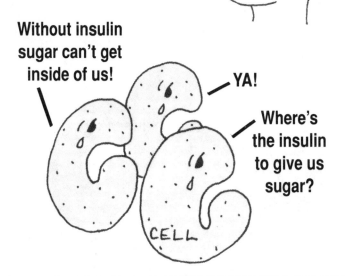

The unhappy cells send messages to your brain that they are starving. That's because all the sugar is outside the cells instead of inside.

Without insulin sugar can't get inside of us!

YA!

Where's the insulin to give us sugar?

Me too!

I need sugar soon!

I'm so tired!

The brain sends a message to eat a lot of food. But the cells still can't eat because there isn't enough insulin to move sugar inside. Then you lose weight.

GROWL!

So the cells are starving, and you are hungry, tired, and losing weight.

The sugar from the food you eat can't get inside your cells and builds up in your blood. More and more sugar builds up until the extra sugar spills into your urine.

DIP TIME READ STRIP

Urine sugar test

Then you have sugar in your urine! That's a sign of diabetes.

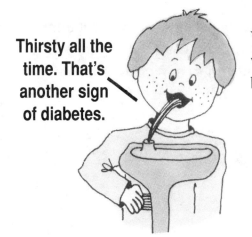

Thirsty all the time. That's another sign of diabetes.

When you have a lot of sugar in your urine, water comes with it from the rest of your body.

Then you have to go to the bathroom a lot. I sure did. That's another sign of diabetes.

And, because you lose a lot of water from your body, you can get very thirsty. Even though you might drink a whole lot, you still feel thirsty.

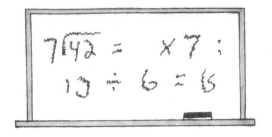

Signs of diabetes happen when your blood sugar is high. High blood sugar can also make things look blurry when you're trying to read or see things faraway.

You can feel very tired too!

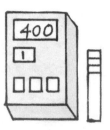

High blood sugar

Unscramble these signs of diabetes.

Write them here.

1. SLOE GIHTWE _____

2. OG OT ETH HBROATOM A OLT _____

_____

3. RHITSTY _____

4. DIRET _____

All the signs of diabetes, like being very thirsty, going to the bathroom a lot, blurred vision, and tiredness will go away after your body gets the insulin it needs. Without insulin, your body cannot grow. When you get the insulin you need, you will grow just fine.

Thanks for the insulin, Cindy! Now we can have sugar and we feel great!

That's because my cells can get sugar to use for energy now that I take insulin!

Name _____ Date _____

Chapter 3.

All About Ketones

When your cells are hungry, your body uses fat instead of sugar for energy. It's not healthy to use or "burn" fat for energy. Burning fat makes ketones. That is when you lose weight.

Ketones build up in your body and spill into your urine. They can act like a poison . . .

. . . and can make you very sick. Sometimes when people get diabetes the ketones make them vomit (throw up), and get very sleepy. Some people feel like they can't breathe well.

A way to see if you have ketones is to urinate (pee) on a special strip. This strip will turn pink or purple if there are ketones in your urine.

Permission to use Mr. Yuk given by the Poison Control Center
of Children's Hospital of Pittsburgh

Make sure you test. Cindy and I do!

It's **very** important to check for ketones at these times:

1. Every morning before breakfast,

2. If blood sugars are high (over 240),

AND

3. When you are sick.

I have ketones this morning, Mom and Dad.

It's also very important to tell your parents or the person taking care of you if you have ketones.

When you have ketones, drink as much sugar-free soda or other diet drinks as you can.

I like to drink sugar-free lemonade!

Fill in the missing word on each of these sentences about ketones.

SUGAR FREE SODA,   STRIP,   PARENTS,
SICK,   FAT,   SICK,   BEFORE,   HIGH

1. Burning _____ makes ketones.

2. Ketones can make you very _____.

3. You can see if you have ketones by urinating (peeing)
   on a special _____.

4. You should check for ketones:

   Every morning _____ breakfast.

   If blood sugars are _____.

   AND when you are _____.

5. Tell your _____ if you have ketones.

6. If you have ketones you

   should drink _____.

Last time when I
was sick I had ketones,
but extra insulin helped
to make them go away!

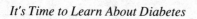

Name _____ Date _____

Chapter 4.

Out of Balance: What Do I Do?

One job your stomach does is to turn the food you eat into sugar. Sugar goes into your blood, and insulin helps it get into your cells. Cells use the sugar for energy!

It is important to have a balance between how much sugar and insulin are in your blood.

When you didn't have diabetes and ate food or sugar, your pancreas made insulin. This kept your blood sugar level in balance.

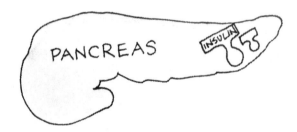

Like a computer that's adjusting things all the time.

When you didn't have diabetes and your blood sugar went up, your body made more insulin! When your blood sugar went down, your body made less insulin.

Connect these sentences with the right ending.

1. The stomach's job is to turn food into   **cells.**

2. Insulin helps sugar get into   **insulin.**

3. Normally, when blood sugar goes up, the body makes   **sugar.**

When you have diabetes, your body can't make insulin. When you take insulin with a syringe, your body can't add more or make less.

Sometimes blood sugar can go out of balance. Your blood sugar might go too high or too low. People who have diabetes have to pay attention to their blood sugar balance every day.

A normal blood sugar should be between 70 and 120 . . .

But blood sugar can go higher right after eating!

High blood sugar: What should I do?

A high blood sugar might happen if you:

Sometimes I don't know why my blood sugar goes high!

- eat too much food

- eat or drink sweet foods

- are sick

- are less active than usual (couch potato)

- don't take enough insulin.

And sometimes a high blood sugar can happen without a reason. When it does, write it down in your daily record book.

First, it is important to tell an adult when you don't feel well.

If you have any signs of urinating (peeing) a lot, thirst, blurry vision, or tiredness, your blood sugar might be too high and your body might be making ketones.

Next, it is a good idea to check your blood for sugar and your urine for ketones.

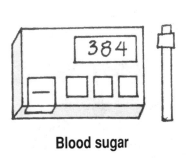

Blood sugar

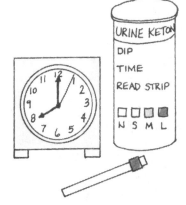

Urine ketones

If your blood sugar is very high or high at the same time every day, you may need to have a change in the amount of insulin you take.

Did you know that if you have ketones and you exercise, your body can make even more ketones! Then you might feel real sick! Ugh!

If your blood sugar is a little high and you don't have ketones, exercise may help to bring down the high blood sugar.

Have your doctor write in the number that is too high for you to exercise. _____

Last time I had high blood sugars, I rode my bike and my blood sugar came right down!

Answer these questions.

1. What are two things you should do if you don't feel well?

   (1)_____

   (2) _____

2. If you're feeling thirsty and tired, what might be happening to your blood sugar?

   _____

   _____

3. Normally, blood sugar before eating is between

   a. 40 and 70

   b. 70 and 120

   c. 120 and 200

   d. 200 and 300

4. Blood sugar usually goes up right after eating.   True   False

5. Exercise is a good way to get high blood sugar down when you don't have ketones.   True   False

6. What is a blood sugar level that is too high for you to exercise? _____

Name _____ Date _____

Chapter 5.

Low Blood Sugar

When the balance between insulin, food, and exercise is upset, blood sugar can go too high (see Chapter 4) or too low.

A low blood sugar might happen if:

- You skip a meal or snack.

- A meal or snack is late.

- You don't eat enough.

- You are or have been exercising a lot.

- You are getting more insulin than your body needs.

Most often, when a low blood sugar happens, your body will give you warning signs.

You might have strong signs or you might not even be able to tell you are low.

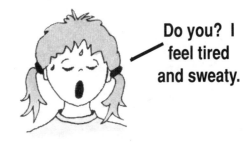

When I get low, I get hungry and shaky!

Do you? I feel tired and sweaty.

When you feel these signs, your body is telling you that you need more sugar in your blood.

If you have had a low blood sugar, you may have felt some of these signs.

Circle the ways you felt.

Shaky

Sweaty

Sleepy

Tired

Confused

Like you can't think

Weak

Hungry

Have a headache

Dizzy

Grouchy

Cold

Heart beating fast

Have a nightmare (at night)

Restless sleep (at night)

Crying for no reason

What you need to do very quickly is:

1. Eat or drink something sweet right away, **AND**

2. Tell someone you are feeling like your sugar is low, **AND**

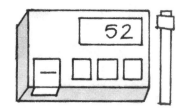

I always tell my teacher and my mom.

3. Test your blood sugar if you can.

What should you eat or drink?

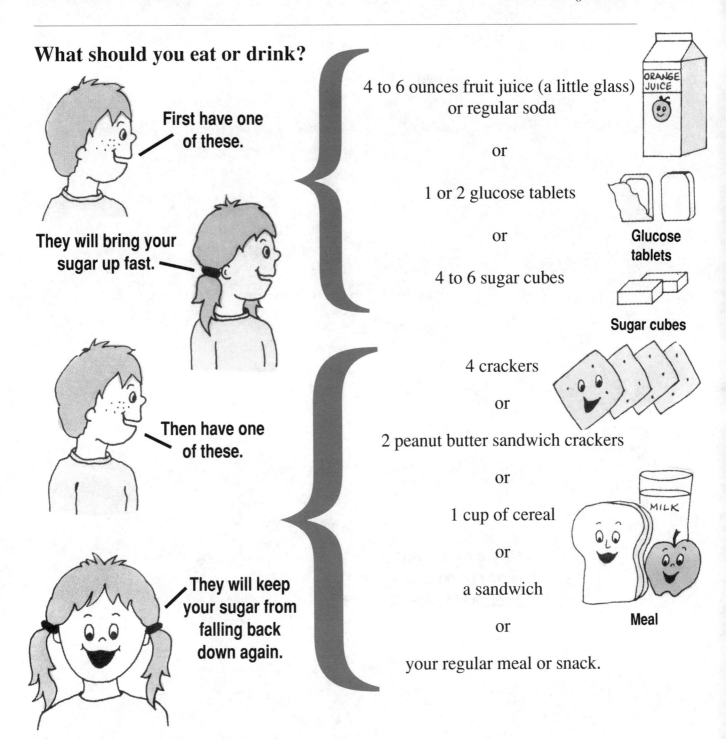

First have one of these.

They will bring your sugar up fast.

4 to 6 ounces fruit juice (a little glass) or regular soda

or

1 or 2 glucose tablets

or

4 to 6 sugar cubes

Glucose tablets

Sugar cubes

Then have one of these.

They will keep your sugar from falling back down again.

4 crackers

or

2 peanut butter sandwich crackers

or

1 cup of cereal

or

a sandwich

or

your regular meal or snack.

Meal

If you aren't feeling better in about 10 minutes, test your blood again (if you can), and eat and drink more if your sugar is still low.

Sometimes a friend can help—if you have told him or her what to do!

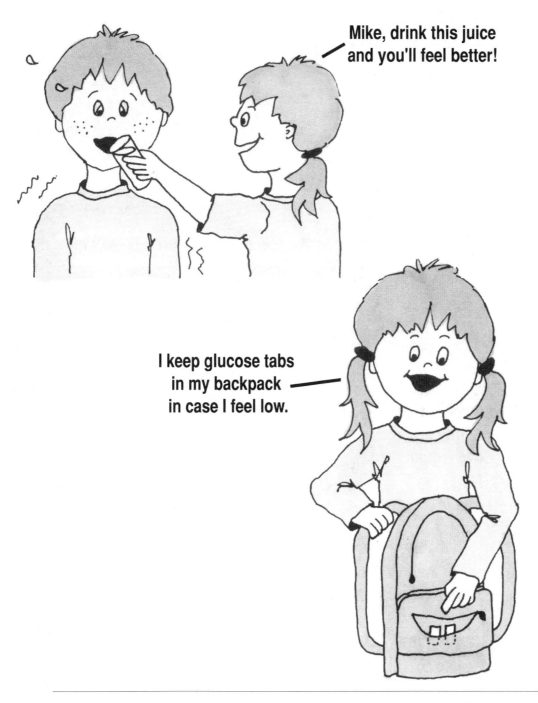

Circle the food that should be used to treat a low blood sugar. Draw an X through the foods that are NOT used to treat low blood sugar.

Diet soda	Coke	Water	Orange juice
Glucose tablet	Celery	Crackers	Sugar cube
Cheese crackers	Sandwich	Peanut butter crackers	
Grape jelly	Sugar-free gelatin		Raisins

In each box draw a picture of a person with the sign of low blood sugar.

Shaky	Sweaty	Sleepy	Hungry	Grouchy

Connect the signs on the left with high or low blood sugar.

Thirsty

Shaky   **High**

Sweaty

Nightmares

Urinating a lot   **Low**

Confused

Grouchy

It is very important to have some kind of sugar with you all the time in case you need it.

Draw a picture of the places you will keep your sugar.
Going to and from school. (Keep it in your pocket, purse, or backpack.)
During gym, recess, or sports. (Keep it in a pocket, helmet, tucked in your sock, or with your teacher or coach.)
On field trips or vacations. (Keep it in your pocket, purse, in the car or bus or give it to an adult who will be with you.)
When playing outside, biking, or exercising. (Keep it in your pocket, taped to your bike, or in your bike pack.)

Fill in the lines below.

When I do these activities: I will keep my sugar in these places.

_____   _____

_____   _____

_____   _____

Sometimes the feelings of low blood sugar can be confused with other feelings, such as being scared or the way you feel after exercise. If you aren't sure if you are low, test your blood.

If you can't test your blood and you feel low, you should *always eat something* anyway, even if you are not sure.

What should you do if you feel you might be low, but you aren't sure?

What kinds of foods would you eat or drink?

Can you guess
what happened
to Cindy?

Name _____ Date _____

Chapter 6.

Taking Insulin

There are many different kinds of insulin. Your doctor will decide which insulin is best for you. Most children with diabetes take two kinds of insulin mixed together.

I take both NPH and Regular insulins.

One kind of insulin, called Regular, looks like clear water. This insulin works very fast. It begins to work in about a half hour after you take it and works hard for about 3 hours.

Other kinds are called NPH or Lente and look cloudy in the bottle when you mix them. They work slowly, over a whole day, and work hardest about 8 hours after they're taken. Your doctor will decide which kind you will take.

Don't forget to mix insulin before you use it. I roll the bottle in my hands to mix it up.

Connect the column on the left with the right kind of insulin.

Works slowly.

Cloudy.

REGULAR

Begins in 1/2 hour.

Works fast.

NPH or LENTE

Clear.

Works hardest in 8 hours.

Insulin is measured in units. The lines on your syringe mark the units. Your nurse will show you how to pull insulin into the syringe.

12 units. That's *exactly* right!

It is **very, very important** to make sure you have the right amount of insulin. If you make a mistake when you are pulling up your insulin, it is important to squirt it out and start all over. If you take the wrong dose, your blood sugar could go too high or too low.

Also, check your syringe for air bubbles. If you have a big, fat air bubble, you won't be getting the right amount of insulin. It's a good idea to have someone else check your syringe before you take your insulin just to make sure everything is OK.

What should you do if you draw up the wrong dose?

_____

_____

You can take insulin in your arms, legs, tummy, and hips. Your doctor or nurse will tell you where your best spots are. It is important to give your insulin in a different spot every day. If the spot where you give your insulin gets puffy or lumpy, the insulin may not work as well as it should. Move to a new spot!

**Pick a new spot everyday!
See where the best spots
are on the drawings below.
There are a lot of them!**

Make sure you pinch up the spot. If you look for a spot where you can pinch a little fat, you will be sure you aren't taking your insulin in your muscle. Insulin might work faster if you put it in your muscle instead of fat.

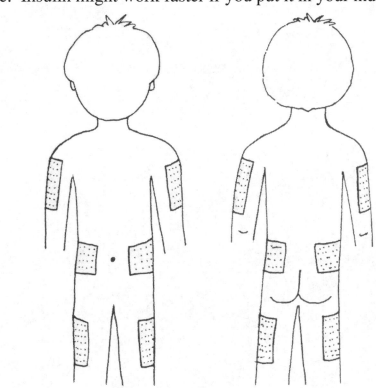

Put the needle straight into the pinched up spot. You can learn to pinch up your arms yourself.

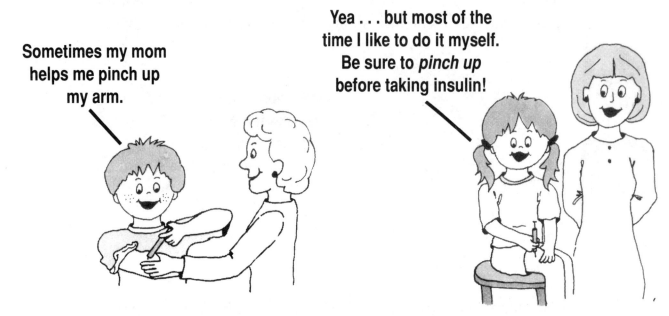

Draw an X on each of the places where you can take your insulin.

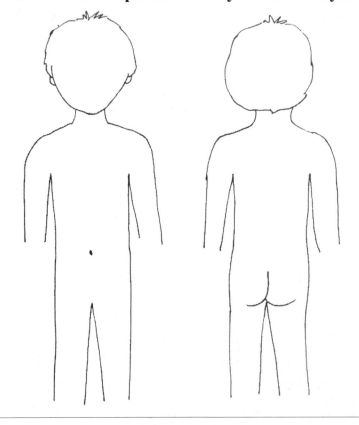

Taking Insulin Crossword Puzzle

Across

2. You don't want these in your syringe.

4. This goes into the syringe.

7. Always take your insulin in different _ _ _ _ _.

8. When you take two kinds of insulin, you learn to _ _ _.

9. The fast insulin that looks like water.

Down

1. Pinch up so you don't get your insulin in a _ _ _ _ _ _.

3. One kind of cloudy, slow insulin.

5. Insulin is measured in these.

6. Do this to your fat when you give your insulin.

7. You pull your insulin into this.

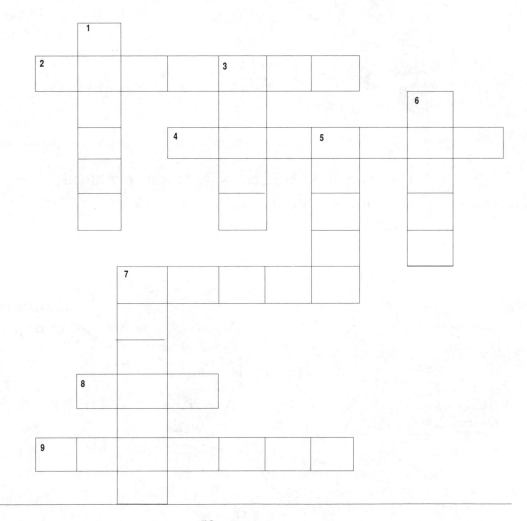

Name _____ Date _____

Chapter 7.

Testing Blood and Urine

One way to help balance your blood sugar is to do blood testing. You can only balance your blood sugar with exercise and food, if you know what your blood sugar level is.

Pricking your finger is very important!

You will learn to prick your finger with a special tool that will help you get a drop of blood without hurting very much.

There are many different ways to test your blood. Your doctor or nurse will help you and your parents decide which is the best way for you.

My new meter is so easy to use!

How to test blood sugar . . .

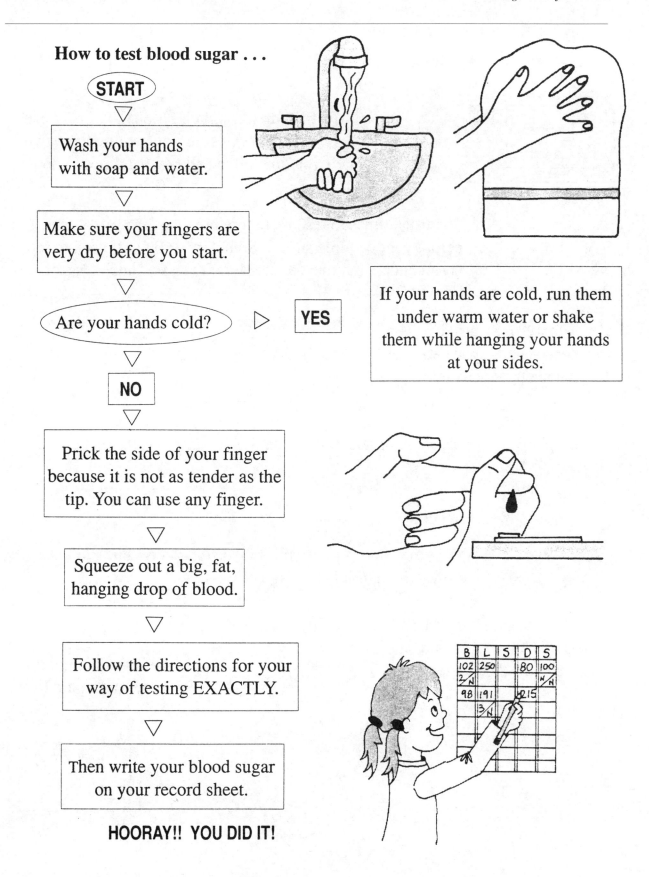

START

▽

Wash your hands
with soap and water.

▽

Make sure your fingers are
very dry before you start.

▽

Are your hands cold?   ▷   **YES**

If your hands are cold, run them
under warm water or shake
them while hanging your hands
at your sides.

▽

NO

▽

Prick the side of your finger
because it is not as tender as the
tip. You can use any finger.

▽

Squeeze out a big, fat,
hanging drop of blood.

▽

Follow the directions for your
way of testing EXACTLY.

▽

Then write your blood sugar
on your record sheet.

HOORAY!! YOU DID IT!

How often to test . . .

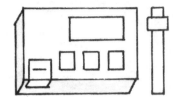

Most children test their blood 2, 3, or 4 times every day. Your doctor, nurse, or parents will tell you how often and at what times to do it.

The usual times to test are before breakfast, before dinner, and before your bedtime snack. Sometimes you will need to test before lunch, but most doctors don't ask for lunch tests on school days.

Test *before* meals because after you eat blood sugar goes up.

Have your doctor or nurse write your times to test here:

_____

You may need to test your blood sugar between your usual times to see if it is too high or too low.

Circle the times you will usually test your blood at home.

Before breakfast   After breakfast   Before lunch   After lunch

Before dinner   After dinner   Before snack   During the night

When I'm not feeling good

Don't forget to write your tests in your daily record book. This will help your doctors, nurses, and parents decide how much insulin you need. You will only be able to keep in balance if you have it all written down.

Name _____ Date _____

Chapter 8.

Healthy Eating

We all should eat foods that are good for our bodies. Children need foods to help them grow and to give them energy. It is especially important for people with diabetes to have healthy eating habits.

**F A T . . . No way!
Not if you eat right!**

The 3 R's of healthy eating are:
- the   **Right** $\boxed{\text{F}}$ oods
- in the **Right** $\boxed{\text{A}}$ mounts
- at the **Right** $\boxed{\text{T}}$ imes.

The Right Brothers!

**The Right Brothers
will help you keep
the balance.**

A dietitian is someone who helps with your meal plan. Your dietitian will explain all about your meal plan.

Keeping the balance between food, exercise, and insulin works best when you stay on a schedule.

What are the "Right Foods"?

Because some foods make blood sugar levels go higher than other foods, you will be given a plan for balancing your meals. The plan will let you pick from these groups.

Bread Group:

Easy for your body to turn into sugar.

Includes: *bread, crackers, cereal, potatoes, rice, peas, corn, pasta*

Fruit Group:

Easy for your body to turn into sugar.

Includes: *apples, fruit juice, bananas, raisins, oranges*

Meat Group:

Turns into sugar more slowly.

Includes: *chicken, cheese, peanut butter, eggs, beef, fish*

Milk Group:

Turns into sugar more easily than the meat group but not as easy as bread and fruit.

Includes: *low-fat white milk, yogurt*

Vegetable Group: Usually doesn't change blood sugar levels much.

Includes: *lettuce, green and yellow string beans, broccoli, carrots, tomatoes*

Fat Group: Doesn't change blood sugar much

Includes: *margarine, nuts, oil, olives, salad dressing*

List these foods under the food group they belong in.

Bananas	Cheese	Eggs	Carrots	Crackers
Nuts	Lettuce	Peas	Peanut butter	Cereal
Milk	Apples	Yogurt	Salad dressing	

Bread	Fruit	Meat	Milk	Vegetable	Fat

When you have diabetes, you take your insulin in a syringe. Your body can't make more if you need it, and you can't shut it off if you have too much.

Since you have diabetes, you should not eat sweet foods very often. Sweet foods (like cake, pie, or candy), send blood sugars up too high, too fast. Insulin can't balance it.

I like to eat cake at birthday parties.

Once in a while, though, it is OK to eat something sweet, such as at a birthday party or after a soccer game.

After a soccer game, I like to eat ice cream.

When you plan to have a sweet, one smart time to have it might be when you plan to be very active. Another time might be when your blood sugar level is low. Your dietitian will tell you how often you can have a sweet food.

We all should watch how much and what kinds of fat we eat. This is even more important for people who have diabetes. Certain kinds of fat (BAD fats called saturated fat and cholesterol) can clog up blood vessels.

We have lots of cholesterol!

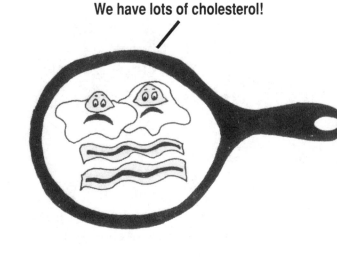

Cholesterol is found in butter, fatty meats, eggs, and cheese.

Saturated fats are found in the same foods as cholesterol but also in some oils such as palm and coconut oil.

Good fats are called unsaturated fats and are in corn oil, olive oil, and vegetable oil.

My mom cooks with margarine and corn oil.

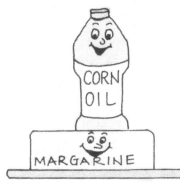

What is the **Right Amount** of food?

You will be eating from all of the food groups. If you are always hungry or can't eat all the food you are given, tell your dietitian so a change can be made in your meal plan.

When you have been exercising and are extra hungry, you should eat more food at meal times. Just make sure you eat the extra food from all food groups.

What is the **Right Time** to eat?

Most children who must take insulin eat breakfast, lunch, afternoon snack, dinner, and bedtime snack. It is important to stay on schedule so meals and snacks can balance insulin.

If lunch is more than 4 hours after breakfast, a morning snack might be added.

If you stay within 1 hour of your normal schedule for meals and snacks, your blood sugar balance should be OK.

Write down the times of your normal schedule.

Activity	Time
Wake up	_____
Test blood and urine	_____
Take insulin	_____
Eat breakfast	_____
Morning snack (if you eat one)	_____
Eat lunch	_____
Afternoon snack	_____
Test blood	_____
Take insulin	_____
Eat dinner	_____
Test blood	_____
Eat bedtime snack	_____

Your schedule is probably a little bit different from mine.

That's because my bus comes earlier than yours.

Yeah, plus I have soccer practice after school.

If you are extra hungry at meal time and want to eat more, what should you eat?

_____

_____

You should try to keep your meals and snacks within _____ (how much time) of your normal schedule.

Name _____ Date _____

Chapter 9.

Exercise Is Fun!

Exercise is fun and healthy for almost everyone.

Circle the kinds of exercise you do!

Running　　Biking　　Swimming　Football　　Baseball　　Softball

Soccer　　Walking　　Hiking　　Track　　　Wrestling　Dance

Gynmastics　　　　　Skiing　　Kickball　　Hockey

Other _____

Exercise keeps your body fit and can be fun. Team sports help people have fun together. When you exercise you will need to know how to keep your blood sugar balanced.

When you are exercising, your muscles use more sugar from your blood. So when you exercise, you MUST EAT MORE food to put back the sugar your muscles used.

Always carry a snack with you. I like raisins and cheese crackers.

If your meal is before exercise, you will need to eat more at the meal. At other times you may need to eat a snack. Here are some ideas for snack foods you can eat before you exercise.

- Raisins

- Fruit

- Sandwich

- Crackers and cheese

- Cereal and milk

- Peanut butter crackers

If you are exercising hard for more than half an hour, you will need to eat a snack to keep your blood sugar from going too low.

I stop to eat peanut butter crackers half way through my soccer game.

If you are planning to do a lot of exercise, like hiking or skiing all day, your doctor might tell you to also take less insulin that day. (We'll tell you more about this in the next chapter.)

Some things you do don't burn much sugar because your muscles don't work much.

Like playing Nintendo, sleeping, or watching TV.

***Don't* exercise when you have ketones!**

If you don't have enough insulin in your body when you exercise, your body starts to break down fat and makes even more sugar to feed the hungry muscle cells. (The cells can't get the sugar, though, because there is not enough insulin.) This is why sometimes when you exercise, blood sugar may go up instead of down! Ketones can also increase.

What is the number that is too high for you to exercise? _____ (See page 32.)

Circle the exercises that help muscles use sugar quickly.

Walking   Biking   Swimming   Playing Nintendo   Baseball

Kickball   Hockey   Basketball   Running   Watching TV

Tennis   Soccer   Sleeping   Talking on phone

My Pledge of Safety

Fill in the blanks.

I promise I will always keep _____ with

(Kind of sugar.)

me in my _____ when I _____.

(Place where you'll carry it.)   (Kind of exercise you do.)

Remember! Always have some fast sugar with you while you are exercising.

Be ready to treat a low blood sugar if it happens. Have fun by keeping it safe!

Name _____   Date _____

Chapter 10.

Balancing It All

Keeping the balance—that's the hard part!

When you have diabetes, three things must
be balanced to keep blood sugar normal.

Circle the 3 things that must stay in balance to keep blood sugars normal.

Insulin   Ketones   Exercise   Thirst   Food

**If you don't
remember, go back
to Chapter 4 to find
the answers.**

When any one of these things goes
out of balance, your blood sugar can
go too high or too low.

In this book we will call a high blood sugar anything over 180 and a low blood sugar anything under 70. Your doctor might give you different numbers that are just right for you.

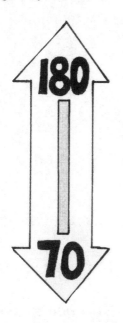

**Anything between 70 and 180 is OK.
A blood sugar of around 100 is normal.**

Circle the meters with blood sugars that are right for you.

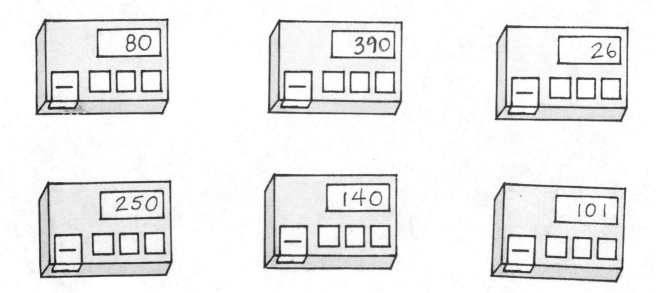

Here is a chart of what you will need to think about every day. On one side are the things that can cause your blood sugar to go up and on the other side, things that can cause blood sugar to go down. When something is happening on one side, you will need to pick something on the other side to balance it.

Makes blood sugar go UP	**Makes blood sugar go DOWN**
Not enough insulin	Too much insulin
Too much food or sweet foods	Not enough food
Stress, cold, flu, feeling upset	Exercise

Here are some things that could happen to make blood sugar go up or down.

- Read the problem.

- Then decide if that problem would make blood sugars go up or down.

- Write down what you could do to balance blood sugar again.

Example:

1. Cindy has a bad cold.

This would probably make her blood sugar go ____**UP**____ .

One thing Cindy could do to keep the balance might be to

____**TAKE MORE INSULIN**____ .

2. Mike is going to play softball.

This would probably make his blood sugar go _____.

One thing Mike could do to keep the balance might be to

_____.

3. Mike wants to have extra pizza at a party with his friends.

This would probably make his blood sugar go _____.

One thing he could do to keep the balance might be to

_____.

4. Some of Cindy's insulin leaked out when she took her insulin.

This would probably make her blood sugar go _____ .

One thing she could do to keep the balance might be to

_____ .

**When you are all done, you can check
your answers on the next page.**

Answers

1. When anyone with diabetes is sick, his or her blood sugar level usually goes **up**. (Body cells need extra insulin when they're sick.)

    If Cindy is not eating much because she's sick, her blood sugar level may be okay. If her blood sugar is too high, Cindy might need to take more insulin. Cindy should not exercise if she's sick. (See Chapter 11, **When I'm Sick.**)

2. If Mike is going to be exercising, his blood sugar level will probably go **down** because his muscles will be using sugar.

    Mike should eat some peanut butter crackers before his game. If he plays hard, he should have juice and crackers between innings.

3. Mike knows that the extra food will probably cause his blood sugar to go **up**.

    If he can plan ahead, Mike and his parents might decide to give extra insulin. Mike also might be able to get some exercise after he eats to keep in balance.

4. Cindy knows that if she doesn't get all her insulin, her blood sugar will probably go **up**.

    She might try to get extra exercise (if she doesn't have ketones). Or she could eat a little bit less if she doesn't feel like eating much.

Keeping the balance isn't easy! Sometimes it's hard to keep on a schedule

The more you know about how to make insulin adjustments, the better you'll know how to keep in balance.

Sleeping late in the morning when you have diabetes just doesn't work! It messes up my blood sugars!

Staying on Schedule

Sometimes you may want to sleep more than one hour past your usual time to get up. One way to get the extra sleep is to get up on time, test, take your insulin, **eat**, and then go back to bed.

Sometimes you might try very hard to keep in balance and it just doesn't work.

Keep trying!! Sometimes you have to try different ways to see what works best for you.

In the summer most children with diabetes eat all
their meals and snacks later to keep in balance.

What is one good way to keep in balance and still sleep in the morning?

_____

_____

_____

Name _____ Date _____

Chapter 11.

When I'm Sick

When you have diabetes and get sick with a cold or flu, your blood sugars can go out of balance. Most of the time when you're sick, blood sugar levels will go up. Also, ketones may be in your urine.

Always tell someone if you vomit (throw up).

Your job when you are sick is to:

1. Tell someone (parent, teacher) that you aren't feeling well.

2. Test your blood sugar every 4 hours.

3. Check your urine for ketones, and tell your parents if the ketone strip is pink or purple. You will need to check every time you urinate (pee) as long as you are sick or until the ketones go away.

4. Drink as many sugar-free drinks as you can.

5. Rest! If you have ketones and you exercise, it can make more ketones.

6. Always take your insulin.

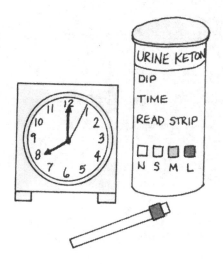

We're always here to help!

Doctor　　　**Nurse**　　　**Dietitian**　　　**Social Worker**　　　**Psychologist**

When I'm Sick . . .

Crossword Puzzle

Down

1. Tell my parents if my urine test turns pink or __ __ __ __ __ __ .

3. __ __ __ __ __ sugar-free beverages.

4. I should test my __ __ __ __ __ sugar every four hours.

5. I check my urine for

   __ __ __ __ __ __ __.

Across

2. When I'm sick, my blood sugar will probably go __ __.

4. When I'm sick, my blood sugar can go out of __ __ __ __ __ __ __.

6. I should always tell some if I __ __ __ __ __.

7. When I'm sick I should __ __ __ __.

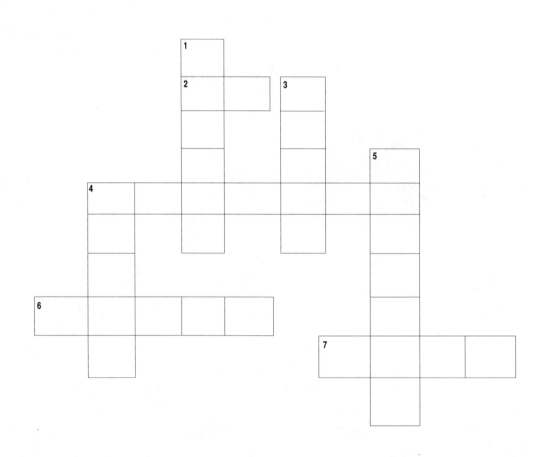

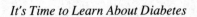

Name _____ Date _____

Chapter 12.

Party Time

Sometimes when parties or holidays come up, you may need to make some changes to keep blood sugars in balance. The very best way of keeping in balance is to plan ahead. Your nurse, dietitian, or doctor will be able to help you plan your day. You can take good care of your diabetes and still do all of the fun things you want to do.

When I'm at a party, sometimes it's hard to pay attention to my meal plan. Mike and I have some tips that work for us.

Boy Scout cookout and award night.

Party Tips

1. Find out ahead of time if a meal will be served, what time, and what foods are planned.

2. Ask if there will be diet soda. If not, take some with you.

3. You may plan to have a sweet food at the party. (If you can, get some exercise later.)

4. If you choose not to have a sweet food, ask for some fresh fruit for dessert or bring your own.

Sleeping Over, Trips, and Vacations

Planning ahead is the key to being able to do all the things you want and still keep your blood sugar in balance.

Cindy and I have more tips for travel . . .

1. Make sure somebody with you knows you have diabetes and can treat low blood sugar.

2. Talk to your doctor or nurse about what to do if you have a problem while you are away.

3. Take more supplies than you think you will need, such as insulin, syringes, and blood and urine testing equipment, in case yours gets lost. Make sure you have plenty of sugar in case you are low.

4. Always wear your identification (ID) bracelet or chain. (See chapter 15.)

5. Keep your insulin in a thermos or cool pack when you travel. Never let it get hot.

Answer these questions.

1. Where is a place you might go away from home?

_____

2. Who might be with you who knows about low blood sugar?

_____

3. What supplies might you take along?

_____

4. Where will you keep your supplies?

_____

5. How will you keep your insulin from getting too warm?

_____

Have fun! But keep it safe!!

Name _____ Date _____

Chapter 13.

Diabetes in School

When you have diabetes, you, your parents, teachers, coaches, and others from your school should have a meeting to decide the best way to manage your diabetes while you are in school.

Together you will need to decide a plan for:

1. *Managing your schedule.*

If you need to have a snack in school, you will have to decide on the best time to eat it. Some children eat their snack in the classroom, while others go to the lunchroom or office.

On gym days, you may need to eat some crackers or a sandwich before gym. If gym is after breakfast or lunch, you can eat more at those meals.

If you have a field trip or activity that might make lunch or snack late, tell someone and take sugar and crackers with you.

2. *Low blood sugar.*

Remember to bring in more glucose tablets, juice, or other food if you use some up.

Some children pack what they call a "low box," which they keep in the teacher's desk. Pack glucose tablets, juice, or raisins and crackers. Keep a box in all your classrooms, the gym, with your coach, and in the library. If you feel your blood sugar is too low, you can eat something out of the box.

If you have a low blood sugar in school, ask your teacher if you can be excused from any test or report for about an hour or so after you feel better. The wait is to make sure you are able to think clearly.

You need to:
1. **Report to the teacher that you are feeling low;**
2. **Eat something sweet; and**
3. **Tell your parents when you get home.**

3. High blood sugar.

If your blood sugar is running high, you may need to ask your teacher for extra trips to the water fountain or bathroom. A note from Mom or Dad to your teacher might help at these times.

Ask your parents for a note if you need one.

Dear Miss Beatle,   *Tuesday*
    Mike's blood sugars are running high this morning. Please excuse him to the restroom as needed.
           Thank you,
           Marcia Adams

---

4. Lunch room eating

Sometimes it is hard to stick to your meal plan when you see other children eating "junk" foods at lunch time.

Pack a lunch that you really like. Choose not to "trade" away your healthy foods. You need them.

Bring home the menu so you can plan what you need at lunch time.

Most schools give out their menu a week or a month ahead of time. Show it to your parents so that together you can decide which meals are good ones for you to eat. Most schools will let you exchange a piece of fruit for the school dessert and have skim or low-fat milk if you ask.

5. Classroom parties

If you know there is going to be a party in school at Halloween, Christmas, or Valentine's Day, you need to plan ahead. You may decide to eat some of the party foods for a special treat.

Most children keep a party box in the classroom or in their locker. Pack foods in your party box that you enjoy and that will be healthy for you to eat.

Party box

If someone brings a birthday treat like cupcakes or cookies, I might decide to have something from my box.

It's smart to make sure you have foods around that you can eat.

Ideas for your party box might be: Diet soda, pretzels, trail mix, peanuts, raisins, vanilla wafers, and animal crackers. Sometimes a friend might bring in a healthy food treat that you and everyone can eat.

What food items will you pack in your party box?

_____

_____

_____

Tell your parents what foods you use so they can keep your party box supplied. And decide, with your teacher and parents, the best way to handle parties in school.

Name _____ Date _____

Chapter 14.

Keep It Safe

Since you are now using syringes and lancets, you have a very important job.

Your job is to keep yourself and other people safe.

Someone could get stuck by your needle or lancet if you aren't careful.

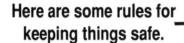

Here are some rules for keeping things safe.

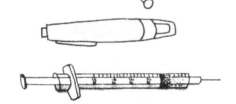

1. Be careful never to stick yourself or anyone else with a used needle or lancet.

• Reason: People can pass germs to each other when needles and lancets are shared.

2. Put all your needles and lancets in an empty plastic milk jug for safety.

• Reason: Little children and others will not get stuck, and you can throw the needles away safely.

Connect the rules on the left with the correct reason on the right.

Don't prick yourself
  with a used needle.

Safely throw out all syringes.

Put them in an empty
  plastic milk jug.

People won't get stuck.

You can throw them
  safely in the garbage.

People can pass germs
  by sharing needles.

Name _____ Date _____

Chapter 15.

Managing on My Own

You are the only one who is with you all the time! So you will need to learn as much as you can about diabetes so you can take very good care of yourself.

Sometimes friends like to learn about diabetes so they can help. Your best friends should know to give you sugar or juice if you have a low blood sugar.

Which friends do you think you'll tell about your diabetes?

_____

_____

_____

You will probably want to learn to give your own insulin and do your own blood tests so you can sleep overnight at a friend's house. (See Chapter 12.)

And you will need to know your own meal plan so you can make healthy choices at school, with friends, and when you play.

Many people can help you take care of yourself, like parents, brothers, sisters, grandparents, friends, your doctor, nurse, and dietitian.

Medical Identification (ID)

When you have diabetes, you always wear a tag or bracelet that says, "I have diabetes." Your doctor or nurse can tell your parents where to buy one.

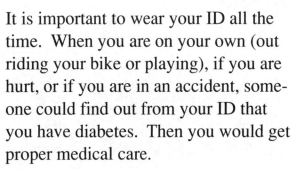

It is important to wear your ID all the time. When you are on your own (out riding your bike or playing), if you are hurt, or if you are in an accident, someone could find out from your ID that you have diabetes. Then you would get proper medical care.

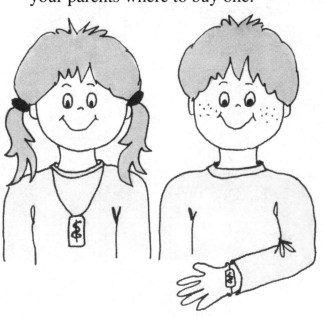

Tips for managing on your own.

1. The more you do for yourself, the more your parents may let you do. You will have shown your parents you are able to take good care of yourself.

2. Tell your parents about any changes you have with your school schedule. You should also tell them if you are having low blood sugar in school or aren't feeling well.

3. Report to your teacher any insulin or blood sugar changes that might affect you in school. For example, if you have a cold and high blood sugar, you may need more trips to the water fountain and bathroom.

4. Always make sure you have something sweet with you. Don't wait for someone to remind you.

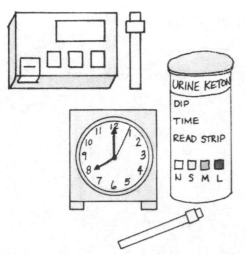

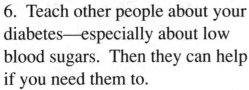

5. Try to do your blood and urine testing without having to be reminded. Moms and Dads really don't like to nag anymore than children like to be nagged. **If you do it first, everyone is happy.** Then, remember to write down your blood sugar and ketone tests.

6. Teach other people about your diabetes—especially about low blood sugars. Then they can help if you need them to.

7. It can be fun to go to diabetes camp in the summer. It's a good place to start to learn to be "on your own" and to be with friends.

8. Remember your ID bracelet or chain!

Pretty soon you will be an expert in taking care of yourself!

Find these items in the hidden picture.

Syringe   Identification tag   Meter   Testing strip

Cells   Insulin bottle   Pancreas

Name _____ Date _____

Chapter 16.

Friends and Feelings

Sometimes it is hard to have diabetes.

Diabetes can make you . . . angry

. . . frustrated

sad. . .

Circle the faces of the ways diabetes makes you feel.

| Scared | Sorry | Bashful | Bored | Forgetful | Curious |

| Confident | Determined | Disappointed | Guilty | Unsure | Disgusted |

| Angry | Frightened | Tired | Sad | Happy | Hurt |

| Idiotic | Jealous | Lonely | Miserable | Puzzled | Satisfied |

| Shocked | Surprised | Thoughtful | Withdrawn |

How does diabetes make you feel?

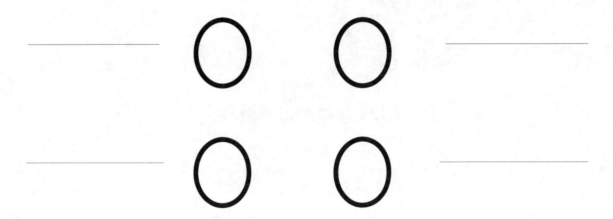

When you have diabetes, sometimes you may wish you wouldn't have to take insulin or do finger sticks. Sometimes you might want to eat or drink foods not on your meal plan, and other times you might not feel like eating things you know you should eat.

You may feel angry or sad. The important thing is to not let your feelings get in the way of taking good care of yourself. The best thing to do is to talk about it with your parents, a good friend, a teacher, or someone who cares. It is OK to feel angry or sad. Everyone who has diabetes feels like you do sometimes.

Scientists are trying very hard to find a cure for diabetes. But in the meantime, staying in shape and taking care of yourself will help you do all the things you want to do in your life. And if you learned a lot from this workbook, then you're on the way!

Date _____

A Letter to my Friend . . .

Dear _____ ,

You may be wondering why I came to the hospital and what is happening to me while I'm here. The doctors told me I have diabetes. The nurses wrote this letter for me to send to you so you can learn a little about diabetes. While I'm in the hospital, I'm learning how to take care of my diabetes, and I'd like to tell you about it.

Before I came to the hospital, I wasn't feeling well. Kids who have diabetes sometimes lose weight, feel tired and thirsty, and may have to go to the bathroom a lot.

Diabetes is NOT a disease like a cold or flu. No one can catch diabetes from me. What happened was my body stopped making insulin. (Insulin helps my body use food for energy.) Now I will need to get my insulin with a syringe. Insulin makes the tired, thirsty feeling go away. It may sound terrible to you to have to take insulin every day, but if it will keep me healthy, it's worth it!

If I have too much insulin, exercise too much, or do not eat enough, my blood sugar level might get too low. That means there is not enough sugar in my blood. I may feel tired, grouchy, sweaty, shaky, dizzy, or confused. If that happens, I need to eat or drink something sweet, like orange juice, soda pop, or sugar tablets. I usually feel better in about ten minutes.

Another way I need to take care of my diabetes is by eating the right amounts of the right kinds of foods at the right times. I will not be eating many fatty or sweet foods. Some snacks I can have are fruit, raw vegetables, and peanut butter crackers.

After I get home from the hospital, I can tell you more about what it was like, if you want to know. My diabetes won't keep me from doing anything. You can call or write to me at the hospital. See you soon!

Your Friend,

Certificate of Accomplishment

This is to certify that

_____

has completed the workbook

It's Time to Learn About Diabetes

_____

(Date)

Signed _____

(Educator)

You've done a great job!
We're proud of you
for learning about how
to take care of yourself!

Answers to Workbook Questions

Unit I.

Chapter 1.

Page 9: 1. brain, 2. stomach, 3. pancreas, 4. lungs, 5. heart

Page 11. diabetes

Page 12. 1. pancreas, 2. no, 3. a cold or flu

Page 17. Take insulin, test blood, eat on time, write down your sugar and urine numbers, test urine.

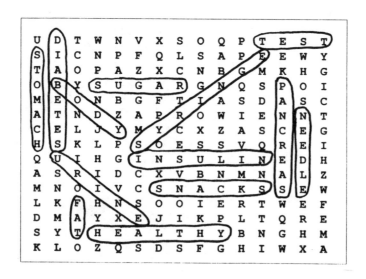

Unit II.

Chapter 2.

Page 21. Pancreas, cells, insulin, sugar

Page 24. Lose weight, go to the bathroom a lot, thirsty, tired

Chapter 3.

Page 27. 1. Fat, 2. Sick, 3. Strip, 4. Before, high, sick, 5. Parents, 6. Sugar-free soda

Unit III.

Chapter 4.

Page 30. 1. Sugar, 2. Cells, 3. Insulin

Page 33. 1. Tell an adult; Check your blood for sugar and your urine for ketones. 2. Blood sugar might be high. 3. b, 4. True, 5. True

Chapter 5.

Page 40. Foods crossed out: diet soda, water, celery,
sugar-free gelatin.
Connect to High: thirsty, urinating a lot
Connect to Low: shaky, sweaty, nightmares,
confused, grouchy

Page 43. Eat something anyway.
Foods with sugar in them.

Unit IV

Chapter 6.

Page 46. Regular: begins in 1/2 hour, works fast, clear
NPH or Lente: works slowly, cloudy,
works hardest in 8 hours

Page 47. Squirt it out and start all over again.

Page 50.

Chapter 8.

Page 57. Bread: crackers, peas, cereal
Fruit: banana, apples
Meat: cheese, eggs, peanut butter
Milk: milk, yogurt
Vegetable: carrots, lettuce
Fat: nuts, salad dressing

Page 61. More from all food groups,   1 hour

Chapter 9.

　　　Page 65.　Circle: walking, biking, swimming, baseball, kickball, hockey, basketball, running, tennis, soccer

Chapter 10.

　　　Page 67.　Insulin, Exercise, Food

　　　Page 68.　80,　140,　101

　　　Page 74.　Get up on time, test, take insulin, eat breakfast, go back to sleep.

Unit V.

Chapter 11.

　　　Page 77

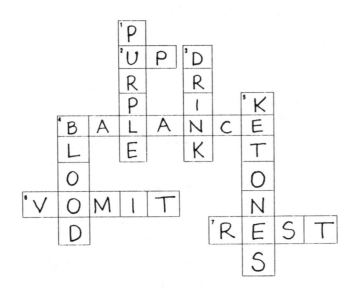

Unit VI.

Chapter 14.

　　　Page 90

　　　Don't prick—pass disease.

　　　Safely throw out—won't get stuck.

　　　Plastic jug—safely throw in garbage.

Hi Again! In this workbook, you learned about taking insulin, and how it helps your body use food to give you energy! We use **Humulin®**, an insulin made by the **Lilly Company**.

There are many kinds of insulin! It's really important to never change the kind of insulin you take unless your doctor tells you to.

The **Lilly Company** helps people take care of themselves by giving information to doctors, nurses, and people with diabetes.

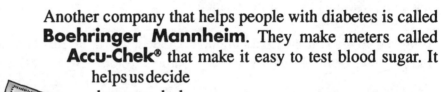

Another company that helps people with diabetes is called **Boehringer Mannheim**. They make meters called **Accu-Chek®** that make it easy to test blood sugar. It helps us decide how to balance our insulin, food, and exercise. They make different kinds of meters so you can pick one that's just right for you! **Boehringer Mannheim** has been making strips and meters to test blood sugar for over 20 years.

If you have questions about your diabetes or about **Humulin®** insulin, call your doctor, nurse, drug store, or diabetes care team. Or call **Lilly** at **1-800-545-5979**.

If you have questions about your **Accu-Chek®** meter, you can call **Boehringer Mannheim** 24 hours a day; every day of the year! The number is **1-800-858-8072**.

Take Care of Yourself!

Bibliography

Betschart J, Siminerio L, Steranchak L, Yeager T: Snips, Spice and All That is Nice. American Diabetes Association Western PA Affiliate, 1987.

Bibace R, Walsh M: New Dimensions for Child Development: Children's Conceptions of Health, Illness, and Bodily Functions. No. 14. San Francisco, Jossey-Bass, December, 1981.

Bigge M: Learning Theories for Teachers, Fourth Edition. Harper & Row Publishers, 1982.

Crider C: Children's Conceptions of the Body Interior. In: Bibace R, Walsh M (Eds): New Directions for Child Development: Children's Conceptions of Health, Illness, and Bodily Functions. No. 14. San Francisco, Jossey-Bass, December, 1981, pages 49-65.

Drash A: Clinical Care of the Diabetic Child. Year Book Medical Publishers, Chicago, 1987.

Fries M: Review of the Literature on the Latency Period. Readings in Psychoanalytic Psychology, Levit M (Ed): Appleton-Century Crofts, New York, 1959, pages 56-69.

Handle With Care: How to Throw Out Used Syringes and Lancets at Home. Environment Law Institute, United States Environmental Protection Agency, Office of Solid Waste, Washington, DC, 1990.

Harrigan J, Faro B, VanPutte A, Stoler P: The Application of Locus of Control to Diabetes Education in School-Aged Children. J Pediat Nursing 24:236-243, 1987.

Puczynski S, Betschart J: Foundation for the Future: Understanding the Student with Diabetes. Greater Pittsburgh Juvenile Diabetes Foundation, American Association of Diabetes Educators, 1991.

Siminerio L, Betschart J: Children with Diabetes. American Diabetes Association, 1986.